Via Crucis

David Butler

Anne
I hope you enjoy

[signature]

⋔ DOGHOUSE

Via Crucis
is published by
DOGHOUSE
P.O. Box 312
Tralee G.P.O.
Co. Kerry
Ireland
TEL: +353 (0)66 7137547
www.doghousebooks.ie
email: doghouse312@eircom.net

© David Butler, May 2011

ISBN 978-0-9565280-6-3

Edited for DOGHOUSE by Noel King

Cover illustration: *Knight, Death and the Devil.* Engraving, 1513
by Albrecht Dürer.
© The Trustees of The Chester Beatty Library, Dublin.

The publisher and poet thank
The Arts Council / An Chomhairle Ealaíon

Further copies available at €12, postage free, from the above
address, cheques etc. payable to DOGHOUSE also PAYPAL -
www.paypal.com to
doghousepaypal@eircom.net

Doghouse is a non-profit taking company, aiming to publish
the best of literary works by Irish or Irish resident writers.
Donations are welcome and will be acknowledged on this page.
For our 2011 publications, many thanks to

Kerry Education Service

Printed by Tralee Printing Works, Monavalley Industrial Estate, Tralee, Co. Kerry

Do mo chlann

Acknowledgements are due to the editors of the following where some of these poems, or versions of them, have been published:

An Guth; The Burning Bush; College Green; ÉIRE / Ireland; Metre; Poetry Ireland Review; The SHOp; The Stinging Fly; The Sunday Tribune; West 47.

This collection was runner-up in the Patrick Kavanagh Award in 2002.

The Arts Council / An Chomhairle Ealaíon awarded the poet a bursary to complete this book in 2005.

The following poems have won individual awards:

Swallows – The Ted McNulty Award, 2000 (for best poem published in Poetry Ireland Review over four issues)
Bray Head – The Tallaght Poetry Prize, 2001
Glassblower – Tallaght / LUAS Award, 2002
Shaving Mirror and Magpies – the Brendan Kennelly Poetry Award, 2002
Chartres Cathedral – the Féile Filíochta Prize, 2005

The following poems have been runners-up:

Francis Bacon at the Hugh Lane – Féile Filíochta (3rd)
Personal Pronoun – Féile Filíochta (3rd)
Absence – Essex Open Poetry Competition (2nd)
Still Life with Oysters – Boyle Literary Festival (2nd)
Caravaggio's 'Taking of Christ' – Edgeworth Literary Awards (2nd)
Wasp – Welsh Open Poetry Competition (3rd)

Preface – by John F Deane

The care in putting together a collection of poems, not just a gathering of poems on disparate subjects, but the sense of a unifying voice and thematic structure, is evident in this book, and the pleasure in recognising such care and following the fugal development, is great indeed. Here is a unit of thought, development, form and imagery. If the Christian myth is currently under attack from the supposed keepers of that myth, David Butler's work demonstrates the on-going, incontrovertible human value that is in the myth, the life, death and mystery of Christ. This, alongside a rich awareness of the pain, longings and love that permeate all human living, combined with an alert and vivid presence to the natural world, offers a poetic that is deeply satisfying on many levels.

The language skills, and the care in the use of words, are obvious from the start. Here is a poet whose knowledge of the poetry of other cultures is intimately connected to his own work, building the treasury that the collection holds. If the overall title is Via Crucis, if the "Interludes" generously placed between the sequences and clusterings, are offered in both Spanish and English, the growing sense that this evokes is a widening of perspective and allusion.

The first, title section, draws on the stations of Christ's journey of pain to the death on the cross, and draws it into the life and sufferings, and death, in a familial setting where we all walk "between desire and regret in a dimensionless present". This is no attempt at alleviation of human dependency but a deepening, a holding to the sense of God's working upon us as a "work of love". So the sequence fills with real tipping points, precisely recalled details, time the colouring, death (though in the context of Christ's suffering and a hint of resurrection) the end. Family, loss, hospital, cancer, funeral - all delicately held, without sentiment, within the story of the Christ, the journey of suffering that was also a journey of love.

The second sequence moves into the area of poetic creation itself. The title poem of this sequence, "Ars Poetica", is a self-ironic, humorous, self-deflating and deeply honest examination of what the artistic endeavour is about. The first Creation myth moves through these poems, linking the work to the first sequence. How insightful, too, the awareness (echoes of George Herbert) that "the love the Creator bore grew more intolerable". The language remains fluid, remarkable, wholly grounded and exciting, as in "the listless left-hand / ivied with paralysis". As in the "Via Crucis" sequence, the "myth" (Christ, Muse) is treated with a heartening realism and a warming relevance to our ordinary, everyday living, the intelligence behind the work a probing human one: stitching "across the incision / with an ugly line of 'ifs'"; the poem "Conditional", as well as carrying through the subject of the mother's death, adds a further dimension of awareness from the perspective of the artist's difficult task.

The final section, "Thoth", is a development of both earlier clusters, adding this other myth, "the ibis-headed Egyptian God of Writing". Here the poet seeks "a lost language" in the things of the created world, God the artist alongside references to Bacon, Rilke, Vallejo, Caravaggio, Dürer. The vision is finely exemplified in a series of poems touching on the created world, and linking to the myth of the Cross, as in "Personal Pronoun": "I am the nail driven through each text / and my shadow stretches, like that of the Cross, / into eternity." Poems like "Wasp", "Chartres Cathedral", "Magpies," "Swallows" (that go "scything and sweeping the hollows, they harvest in / The last sheaves of light. And then they are gone, / And with them the summer") exemplify Butler's closeness to reality; this is not poetry merely skimming the surface of our myths, it is a poetic rooted in everyday things, and in the world about us. The poem based on Caravaggio's Taking of Christ admirably ties the several strands of the book together.

All in all it is a brilliantly conceived and finely mastered collection, satisfying on several levels. Here is a voice and a poetic strength to be heartily welcomed into the contemporary poetic endeavour.

John F Deane, 2010

Contents

Part I Via Crucis

Interlude:

Part II Ars Poetica

Note: All translations by David Butler

Part I

VIA CRUCIS

Gott war schwer zu überreden;
und er drohte ihm, statt zu gewähren,
immer wieder, daß er sterben werde.

Rilke *

* God was hard to persuade;
and, instead of acceding, He threatened him,
again and again, that he would die.

'Adam',
from Neue Gedichte.

Condemned

Mortality Sonnet

The applause was hesitant at first,
nobody quite sure whether or not
the corpse would get up again.
It lay supine, cheek to the dust,
the spine twisted into an attitude
somewhere between relief and agony.
There was a grimace underlying the jaw
so ambivalent it was almost a grin;
it might have been taken for sarcasm.
So the handclaps were sporadic to begin with,
until all at once it became apparent
what daring theme the Artist had conceived.

That's when the Angels burst into wild applause.

The Cross

Vanitas

The year has skipped away like a stone
across the surface of days.
At a distance, what can be seen
stretching out before, stretching out behind,
is a benign, unbroken stillness.
But there is a sound of rushing nearby,
where our bodies are immersed;
a sound like God's hatred.

Distant years have the appearance of marble.
We think that, once we've carved dates into them,
they stand still, take on permanence.
We think to make them coincide with calendars.
But instead they turn and eddy,
slip the shackles of our dates
and glide inexorably past us.
Our projects are carried with them, shades
lacking to the end in resolution.

For years are too large for us.
There is space in a year
for all the people of the Earth,
walled between desire and regret
in a dimensionless present.
Time is God's breath, and it withers us.
We shrink and writhe before it
like sheaves left too near the furnace.

But God says, *this is love.*

First Fall

Puberty
after Munch

She is dwarfed,
the shadow looming on the wall
like a knowledgeable familiar.
Her body is already become strange
with incipient tumours of sex,
with blood-letting.
Her limbs are grown too long for her.

Her arms are too long,
but they cross so delicately
she might be carved from soapstone.

Mother

Mother

Who would have imagined this awkward dance:
you heavy, almost crippled,
me looking away, smiling to my father
as we ease you back towards the bed;
the flippant whiz of the morphine pump
and the grotesque rattle, a drowning
three days before you drowned.

That was the hottest day of the year;
the air throbbing with the sounds of a fête,
a tortoiseshell frittering at the window.

Simon of Cyrene

V
Médecin sans Frontières
i.m. Gary Butler

They say we looked alike,
even down to the gesture.
A tint in the iris, otherwise
people might have mistaken us.

You grew intimate with Death,
played games against Him, while
Time, gone crazy,
ticked away at your blood.

Might they have mistaken us?
To be impelled
to shoulder such loads –
a thing I talked about.

Veronica

VI

Birthmark

It might be a bruise or a weal,
a purple swelling brought up
by an almighty blow to her face.
If so, the slap
was dealt while the pale form
still waxed inside the matrix.
Then a childhood stigma,
a port-stain, an indignant sediment
that crusted, later, into mockery
of the body's uneasy tumescence;
of the blood's incessant tattoo.
Christ!

Second Fall

Shaving Mirror

The illusion, in its concave retina, is
virtual, magnified and upright,
which shows the treachery of words.
Rather say the image exaggerates
with the precision of satire.
It is a theatre of parallax;
a moving circle, centred on the eye;
a mercurial portrait, to which
time, a third-rate artist
who can't leave well-enough alone,
returns, morning after morning,
to rework line and hatching
with ever coarser charcoals,
until the figure is botched, once for all,
to caricature.

Women of Jerusalem

VIII

Visiting Hour

*Have you observed that the one behind moves what he
touches? The feet of the dead are not wont to do so.*

Inferno, Canto XII

Down the long torpor of corridors
the grey men echo;
each has the face of a bankrupt.
Asked, they wince a new complaint.

Spirit has been sterilised in the panoptic
of chrome and enamel.
The diagnostic air
is merciless as a chemistry lesson.

Outside, the day moves, rush hour to rush hour,
but viewed as if through gauze.
Inside are the tones of the confessional.
The wards are poorhouses, named for saints.

But all bursts abruptly to life at the hour
when the bluff and sanguine circulate
their evasive optimisms. No doubt they hope
there is nothing quite as contagious.

Third Fall

infestation:

when
it has once
nested inside the body
cancer develops a hunger for interiors
methodical as a night spider it
probes the intimate body and
insinuates its waxen egg
then it hides

later with
incubation the host
stares out from hollow eyes
shaven-headed victim
of a pogrom

hatched out
cancer has no use
for the wasted organ
it creeps back to its lair
heavy with new
eggs

and waits

Stripped of Garments

X

Changing Rooms

Enclosing space, time becomes enclosed.
Half-awake, you hear the flutter of wings
against the bedsit's economic confines.
Feathers accumulate in every vertex
until the air is stagnant with discarded days.
But time has flown the trap.
If a body has left its bird-like impression,
it's the fragile relic of preferences.

So, changing one room for another
should be a form of resurrection,
or at least, a probation of the will.
On walls and shelves, the life chosen
bears witness, like a cave-dweller's daubs.
You've no more chosen life than these dimensions.

Nailed to the Cross

XI

Solar
Il sole non vide mai l'ombra – da Vinci*

The sun is all but blind.
All light flees the clamour of its skin.
Its sight has dimmed from straining
interstellar dark for the merest glimmer
of another sun. But nothing answers.
The sun's blank eyeball is backed
by a retina empty of image.
Only the stars' eternally distant braille
and sycophantic rings of flint and dust
scintillate with reflected glyphs.
The sun calls into universal silence
until it has lost its voice to cosmic deafness.
It dies, knowing nothing beyond the slow orbit
of satellites, cogs of a clock unwinding.

* The sun has never seen shadow

Dies

Cadavre Exquis*

Dawn finds the exquisite corpse
and grafts to imperfect contour
the facsimile of a new day.
It is a subtle game.

Once it is reanimated,
the corpse mustn't become aware
of the blue tissue
that grafts over the joins.

Not until the game is stopped.

This is the moment
when all the sutures come undone,
when the ensemble hangs free,
a rag doll for memory to play with.

** Literally 'exquisite corpse', a collaborative game played
by the Surrealists to generate unpremeditated images.*

Taken Down

XIII

Pietà

What remains, then,
after the curtain has dropped,
and the light died?
The scaffolding
is soon taken down,
the props packed away
with the sheets, the costumes.
Grief doesn't long outlive
the hasty burial.
Even the words,
the unique testament
that make up a life,
will soon become equivocal.
In a few hours
it will be hard to believe
this cage of humanity
ever walked.

Burial

Funeral

The wet earth yawned
open its bevelled maw.
An ochre seepage gathered
in runnels on its floor.
No. No. No.

And the box bumped along
on shuffling shoulders
through the respectful gap
left by the mourners.
No. No. No.

No. No. No. But
they failed to hear. Or they heard.
The bowed heads of the congregation,
the priest with his words.

No. No. No, said the corpse,
inside the gravel bed,
No. No. No, – a gaping silence,
the voice left the dead.

Interlude

Naturaleza Muerta con Ostras

La toalla se empapa de la lucha:
la navaja avanzando a tientas
para frotarse un fulcro.
A medida que cede la cutícula
los interiores de nácar
babean salmuera.
Una torsión brusca de acero
raja pues la tosca paleta
en cielo y reflejo.

¡No tengamos nada que ver con los preliminares!

Quedémonos contentos de momento
que el ojo pueda atracarse de cuanta desnudez
se avergüence entre las piedras de hielo.
Detrás del verde frío del vino
una canasta de cascos descartados
podría convertirse en escápulas.
Mas ya estamos pendientes
del instante agudo cuando cada tono
se deshaga en salinidad.

Still Life with Oysters

The towel is damp with struggle;
elemental steel inched inward
to fret out a fulcrum.
When the cuticle yields,
saltwater dribbles out
from each nacreous interior.
Then the blade's quick twist
cleaves the roughshod palette
into sky and reflection.

We would know nothing of preliminaries.

We content ourselves, momentarily,
that the eye glut itself on such nakedness
as palpitates upon the rock-ice.
Behind the wine's green chill
a basket of discarded plaques
could masquerade as scapulae.
But already we're impatient
for that acute instant when all tone dissolves
into salinity.

Part II

Ars Poetica

Ars Poetica

I hadn't seen her in fifteen years.

I'd grown so used to her absence –
the memory more vague
with every backwards glance –
that I'd begun to doubt
I'd ever met her in the first place.

Then out of the blue she turned up,
middle-aged, lecherous,
slovenly in her dress.
A layer of cheap powder and
a waft of gin on her breath.

The grin I gave her must have revealed
how far into life I'd waded, wondering:
'Is this what the Muse has come to
that I once mistook for Beauty?'
She grinned back at me, quick as the thought:

'*Your* Muse,' she winked.

Transgression

The story is too perfect:
How a Creator, filled with sad affection for his
creation, fashioned him a Paradise. The charge
was that he only be content there, and not think of
leaving. And how the creation, growing restless,
made to leave. *Step outside this perfection I made
for you and you will be made imperfect.* The creation
scarcely paid the warning heed. *Outside of here is
death, is ageing.* The creation shrugged and took
a further step. The Creator, transfixed by this
disregard, gazed at the creature he had made.
A third time the voice rang out. *And everlasting
punishment, Hell, if you defy me.* But the creature
walked away, stooped, died, gave birth to a race.
And with every step, with each new transgression,
the love the Creator bore grew more intolerable.

      The Devil was horrified. Finally, he came to
Man, and whispered the only word he could find in
the arsenal of his guile that might tempt him, might
serve to diminish this perfect love. *Repentance.*

Comhrá na Tríonóide

Is mé ar seachrán san coláiste ar maidin
do bhaineas ana-thaitneamh as mo dhíchuimhne
nuair a thugas faoi deara
go rabhas ag caint liom féin
fad is ag falróid a bhíos.
Trí cheist le freagairt dá bhrí sin:
Cé bhí ag caint? Cé bhí ag éisteacht?
agus in ainm Dé,
cé bhain aoibhneas as an staid sin?

Trinity Colloquy

And I wandering between Faculties this morning,
I got a kick out of my own forgetfulness
when I realised
I'd been talking to myself
all the while I was walking.
Three questions arise out of this:
Who was doing the talking?
Who the listening?
And in God's name
who got such a buzz out of it?

Absence

*L'homme est l'être par qui le néant vient au monde.**

Sartre

Of the words that separate us from animals
absence is the most disruptive and immediate.
It is colourless, weightless.
It has no home in the world
but is carried parasitically,
voracious as the hollow of memory.
It is odourless and silent.
Its slow accumulation tilts, by degrees,
the scales that weigh up
whatever it is we call ourselves.
It is the amputee's void sleeve.
It is furniture's melancholy.
It is Death's soundless anthem.

There is a world of difference
between a blank wall
and the wall from which a portrait
has been removed.

** Man is the being through which absence enters the
world.*

Wine

Veiled muse, votary of all things profane,
so far from vine as plainsong from choir,
who pressed you into this cloister of glass?
Who set this seal on your rubicund singing?

Let me draw out your recusant soul
from the cell of its dark confinement
till it bursts this green calyx, this sanctuary lamp,
and pleasures the air with decanting.

What cardinal shame so confined your bloom
and furled up your tenebrous petals?
One by one let my mouth open them
and know again the fruit of your prodigal interior.

River Gods

for my sister Joan

I'd always been horrified
by the thought of River Gods;
their webbed skin, their
breath of must and decay,
their muscles, quirky as eels.

Fetid creatures were sure to live
in the long tresses of beard
that dangled from their mouths,
glutted and soft with
their dull monotony of swallowing.

And to think of the bathing nymph,
how the young flesh must recoil
at the first touch, before she is dragged
down, that set my skin writhing.
I was wrong: River Gods

are harmless creatures, too awkward
to walk on dry land without stumbling.

Siren Song

Heart, how long ago did you crawl
inside this carapace, like a hermit crab
or livid cephalopod, to squirm out
your muted tattoo of mortality
through the planks of its obscene interior?

Where did you learn your shy intimacy
with Time? The only retort you give,
the dark plumes that disturb the sediment
like feather-dusters while you recoil
further inside the chamber of rhythms.

How strange it is that, talking of Love,
I'll sometimes lay a hand, here, like a shadow
on the water's surface. At the first disturbance
you are gone, Heart, your departure
momentarily obscured in blue, cumulus inks.

Francis Bacon at the Hugh Lane Gallery

I

The August light anonymous
and warm. Buses droning up past the Rotunda,
or idling next to the IERNE, taking the sun.
Inside the Garden of Remembrance
the cross of water, ripple-free
and Lir's children rising still.

II

    as nightmare
maremouth open air –
less scream
dissslocate soundless

             Fface of
           man ?) in cyanide aSPHixiate blue
               drowNEd, livid, blurrrr
             surfaceglass shadow

    ccccrawling cross redness
      rawred, bare: arid torso
straightjacket limblessness
and the Umbrella !
  as though as though as though

           Studio searchlight; an eye
           on oval operating table
           bare flesh contorted
           and around it zinc white
           curves antiseptic rail

heheheads in   series
     mMegaccccccephaLlous
   three   tryptich333
deformedistortediseased
   Bbrow jawbone a

III

Outside, again.
The light momentarily disorients,
the air warm and noisy. A smile,
ambivalent, in what might be termed
apologetic admiration:
And he was from Dublin, too,
though you'd never believe it.

Insomniac

Silence is aspirate.
It fills his room with
whispering.

Night tosses about
restless as dark foam,
and mind flits bat-like
from thought to thought.
In all this movement
only the body strives
for perfect stillness.
The body,
weary as a vessel
in which the ballast has shifted.
The head reels with the problem
of finding a lie
to accommodate its list.
The head reels, and the eyes
ache at the spin of hours,
until daylight grounds
mind, eye, body
on shallow sandbank.

Sunlight discovers him
rising to his feet,
a shipwrecked man.

Stroke

Death touched her.
Now one half of her
belongs to Death.

Flesh waxed inert.
She can do nothing
to quicken its pallor.

Even the lightest
task has grown heavy:
dressing; undressing.

Nerves are phantoms;
the listless left-hand
ivied with paralysis.

Her body is in eclipse;
an eye rages, indignant
at such stupidity,

and tongue is dull to toll
how a corpse has embraced her
and drags, endlessly, downwards.

Bray Strand
for KTB

The sun dangles nets in the gelid water.
Light shivers, and scribbles fine filaments
whose shadows flit over the sea floor.
Still, the ebb will slip them, leaving
a drying cerebellum of sand engraved
with nothing but the memory of motion
beneath the wind's slow erasure.

So days slip from us. The soul's nets
play in the flow and ebb of hours
and cast their memory in languages
too coarse and rigid ever to catch
the nuance of living. We think
to fix love, that is so fugitive,
and in words inscribe its epitaph.

Conditional

i.m. my mother, Betty Butler

Death stole up,
wearing the mask of a surgeon.
He cut out our word 'when'
saying that it had grown malignant,
then stitched across the incision
with an ugly line of 'ifs'.

I doubt, up to this point,
that any of us had realised
how clumsy this word is,
how little to be trusted.

Glassblower

It is as though an incandescent swarm
has clustered, on a spindle of his breath,
to fabricate a hive
in the hot globe of amber.
It's as though the air is given hands,
cupping the molten bubble thrown out
by his steady lung, crafting
the dull red sun until it sets,
like a premonition of winter,
into the fragile geometry of glass.

The Clown

Gloucester is kneeling.
    He is straining the wind
for the garrulous sea,
    the dementia of gulls.

    He can no longer reason
into three dimensions
    the co-ordinates of
a sensible world.

The Globe has shrunk to a drumroll
that vibrates beside him.

    Now he will end it.

Interlude

Odaliscas

La huerta de rosas se llena de celos:
cada flor es la boca de una sinvergüenza
que hace pucheros y luego despliega
blanca de enaguas, carmesí cachondo.

He aquí unas mortíferas rivalidades
en los perfumes que atrapan zumbidos
a lo largo de la tarde lánguida; mas de repente
he el choque de la inocencia inesperada.

Lo más cruel es el decaimiento continuo
de las viejitas que desmayan al suelo;
de las marchitas envidiosas que aún se pegan
a las rodillas de sus calvos estambres.

Odalisques

The rosebed is heavy with rivalries.
Each head, the mouthing of concupiscence;
intimate whites, reds dark as sin,
a pout, then a slow undressing.

There are deadening jealousies abroad;
languorous perfumes that trap insects
all through the long afternoon. But here,
the disclosure of unfurled innocence.

Cruellest is the discarding of petals,
the fall to earth of the faded;
the jaded glance of the envious, who
cling to the knees of bald stamen.

Part III

Thoth

Thoth

The prints of a moorhen
on the soft mud by a river,
(so the philosopher says),
form no more than the trace,
the purest absence,
the hollow cast of a creature
that, (we only suppose), laid them.

But the poet, (if he can be believed),
says he sees a lost language,
regular, cuneiform;
a pattern of runes and glyphs,
no less the text, because we cannot read it,
than the testament of some lost race
that awaits its Rosetta stone.

Undecided,
pulling between pure absence
and a silent alphabet,
these black prints,
set into the soft mud of the page.

Thoth: the ibis-headed Egyptian God of Writing

Personal Pronoun

I am the first person, singular,
a girder, an exclamation mark.
I am a bone, a yellowed femur;
capitalised, in the Ionic style,
I have grown durable, the single column
that outlives the passing of empires.
I am a phallus, a stele,
a digit, raised in admonition.
In the literature of every age
my fine-honed identity is indispensable.
I am the nail driven through each text,
and my shadow stretches, like that of the Cross,
Into eternity.

Swallows

Scythe-wings slide from the low vaults, calling,
fall through the line of sight, swing wide,
and, tight to the lawn, race their shadows.
Gracing an arc, a long drawn, mower's sweep,
the lithe blades wheel and leap at once upwards,
    deep,
deep in the blue air.

Chatter thrown wide over unploughed winds,
they gather high, then scatter in heady reels
to sow their sky-notes, peels, thin chips of sound,
till they halt, crest, fall again low to ground
and reap the long hours that have grown there
over the fields.

The seasons turn, the dusk-silted eaves fall dumb,
shunned by their feints of leaving, flights in
    shadow.
They weave and scatter at nightfall, gather their
    numbers
and scything and sweeping the hollows, they
    harvest in
the last sheaves of light. Then they are gone,
and with them the summer.

Pheasant Plucker

That dappled wood-kerne,
ducking and diving, eking
an edgy living from briars,
thrusting through jagged hedges
a phthalic head, red-eyed
on coarse-grained clockwork,
cocky as Jagger and just
as cantankerous, would be,
you would think, fair game –
such pride is proverbial.

After the throat-crake
flight is an eructation:
a bowl of feathers tossed up
in a burst of inadequate wings
that haul the great tail, the
cumbersome bustle some twenty yards
before he falls back
amidst the stubble
into his strut –
where females flock to him!

The Silent People

It's an untold story, cast
into gaunt figures
on a bank
indifferent to their passage.

Those years the drills were
Famine stalked
the land expelled them
in dry retches.

With wind bellying
the hoar-canvas
of westward sails,
they made bare ballast

in the holds of coffin ships
in whose wakes
the throats of the harbours
constricted.

Note Found in a Volume of Vallejo

Santiago was the bell-ringer in Santiago de Chuco,
Vallejo's hometown. Though blind, Santiago was afraid
of the dark.*

The dusk, hesitant,
laying cold hands to the cheek.
The hour has stopped breathing, or
exhales slowly, downwards.
Then a flutter, felt more than heard,
an urgent palpitation of the air.
It is as though somewhere a wing is trapped.
Silence follows this, extending sightlessly,
by touch, its taut web,
listening.

Listening
for an echo,
a door closed, a voice,
a footfall, silence diminishing distance.
There is an unreal moment
– a clock about to strike –
then all at once, low, sonorous,
the air comes alive with resonant bronze.
Santiago's church-bell has started awake, tolling
darkness, visible;
darkness, visible.

*Found on A volume of Vallejo

Caravaggio's *Taking of Christ*

I

Is it the lantern or the mounting darkness
that has etched lines of moment
deep into the foreheads of both men?

Eyes that stare through the present
and into a Godless future;
eyes cast down to fingers' quiet braid.

What holds them one to another?
Viewed *sub specie aeternitatis*
every betrayal subtends fulfilment.

The parables have said as much:
in the embrace, the denouement;
in death, the seed.

In any case these arms are not his
that grasp, that seize *trompe l'oeuil*
in casques of reflective armour.

Avatars of light and night cast
together in eternal chiaroscuro,
who is finally the more dejected?

II

The primal scene is framed
between Artist and Evangelist.
The beloved one turns away
on the side of the saved.
Agape, ready to crow,
his hand is a bird taking fright.
The other looks on,
tendering complicit light
from the company of soldiers.

III

What is it that *His* eyes express,
downcast onto the intimacy of fingers?
That nothing is so heavy as foreknowledge?
He could inform this disciple
that the coming day
will see them both hanged.
But the fingers intertwine,
the eyes remain wordless.
Disappointment? Love?
Infinite solitude?

Wasp...

... leaves its paper-lantern nest,
a painted samurai.

September has filled it
with the jitters.
When it crawls the globe
of a pitted windfall
wings fidget
to right its stumbling.

Its antennae are
nerve ends.

A humour
of the grey air
has maddened the venom
inside its double-
jointed abdomen:
black-bile;
yellow-bile.

It can sense the end.

Now it turns
kamikaze:
launching
into one last
delirious flight
it is
fanatic,
frenetic,
simply dying
to fall upon the sword.

Dürer Engraving, 1513

Strange company to keep, Sir Knight,
though the eyes are fixed dead ahead,
and the horse is caught in mid-stride
at the impregnable instant of return,
beneath the battlements. Here is the paradox:
for outside of the streaming hour
neither Devil nor Death has demesne.
Noseless Death, the importunate suitor,
mounted hard alongside, and behind
like pestilence, the Devil's faecal smell.

Below is the familiar device, set as a milestone:
A a gallows under which **D** has taken refuge.

Chartres Cathedral

Faith made these vaults ascend to touch,
like Dürer's hands, at the apex of veneration.
Now, the dimensions are the fossils of that faith.
Now, who steps into the flag-stoned interior
is blinded for a time by afterimage –
opaque echo of the sun's profanity.
Eye must accommodate to angular half-light
leaning through texts of glass, and lapidary stillness
suspended from the thorax of the great nave.
Nothing breathes. Or is it that we have lost the skill
to see in the chancel's crustacean intricacies
anything but dead form? Perhaps it was always so:
the soul a hermit crab that rummages through exteriors
cast in the image of faith, world without end.

Bray Head / Bray Head

Rocks are nouns,
hedral, obstinate;
but the sea is all verb.

Today the subjunctive mood is on her.
She is mights, woulds,
every sort of conditional.

Today's skin is supine;
the undertow
tenses and dilates.

Wrack and tackle
wither on the shore
of last night's imperatives.

The sea is all verb.
Before her, our pronouns crumble
into predicates.

Magpies

Precariously dropped
into the high crooks and snags
of the most restless boughs,
the sprigs and osiers
of their slapdash nests
will barely stand the first test
the wind tosses their way.
(The ground is littered with earlier failures.)

Magpies don't give a damn.

Chattering and cackling
– more hyena than bird –
a clownish convocation
in black and white habit
capers across the lawn,
tails up like exclamation marks.
Slapstick harlequins,
they are as raucous as drunks,
as cheeky as novices
playing truant
from some monastic order.

But the hysterical songbird,
flitting under the hedge,
trills a staccato alarm.
She cries out
that these squabbling comics
don the hood of the executioner,
the black cowl of the terrorist.
She has learned,
in a plundered eggshell,
in the downy relic of a fledgling,
that it was masked antics like these
who first brought death
into the garden.

Death-Watch

One year is
   all the doctors gave.
Days,
   he envies everyone
their hoard of time.
   Past has no substance.
Future, gangrenous,
   is to be severed.
Mornings,
   solitude rises with him
like an allegory.
   Friends shy away.
He's begun to resemble
   ambition's corpse.
And nights,
   his mind is a miser's,
tormented by rumour:
   by the ticking
of the clock...
   by the tickling
of the clock...
   by the tricking
of the clock...
   by the trickling
of the clock...

Epitaph

These are not days, they are shadows
flitting over the too familiar ground,
dry and rubble-strewn,
where our choices are buried.

These are not days, these shades,
tremulous, mere changes of light.
Quiet as thieves, as witnesses,
they slip past in silent legion.

Count them up and they come to years,
but years empty of substance.
They are the dry husks of our lives,
the whisper inside the hourglass.

Days are not the coinage of will,
as once we imagined.
One day they rise like locusts,
to devour us.

Postscript

Postscript

The Angels return, not like migratory birds,
but laden down with archaeological equipment.

Their task is to disinter the past,
scraping marl from rotten coffin-lids
and prising open airless mausoleums.

It is worth seeing what they can glean
from lettering that time has all but erased;
from a femur; a jaw; a single molar;
from the merest handful of dust.

Their bane is the paupers' plot,
the cholera pit, the ossuary
where entire shifts are taken up
sorting, comparing, classifying,
putting numbers to disarticulated bones.

What is it that the Angels learn
remembering corpses?

A native of Dublin, **David Butler** has lived and taught in the Seychelles, Australia, Spain and Venezuela. He has won numerous literary awards, including the Ted McNulty and Feile Filíochta for poetry and the Maria Edgeworth (twice) for the short story. His novel *The Last European* (Wynkin de Worde) was published in 2005. Other published works include *Selected Pessoa* (Dedalus Press), *An Aid to Reading Ulysses* (Dublin City Libraries / James Joyce Centre).

Also available from DOGHOUSE:

Heart of Kerry – an anthology of writing
from performers at Poet's Corner, Harty's Bar, Tralee
1992-2003
Song of the Midnight Fox – Eileen Sheehan
Loose Head & Other Stories – Tommy Frank O'Connor
Both Sides Now - Peter Keane
Shadows Bloom / Scáthanna Faoi Bhláth – haiku by John
W. Sexton, translations, Gabriel Rosenstock
FINGERPRINTS (On Canvas) – Karen O'Connor
Vortex – John W. Sexton
Apples in Winter – Liam Aungier
The Waiting Room – Margaret Galvin
I Met a Man... Gabriel Rosenstock
The DOGHOUSE book of Ballad Poems
The Moon's Daughter – Marion Moynihan
Whales off the Coast of My Bed – Margaret O'Shea
PULSE – Writings on Sliabh Luachra – Tommy Frank
O'Connor
A Bone in my Throat – Catherine Ann Cullen
Morning at Mount Ring – Anatoly Kudryavitsky
Lifetimes – Folklore from Kerry
Kairos – Barbara Smith
Planting a Mouth – Hugh O'Donnell
Down the Sunlit Hall – Eileen Sheehan
New Room Windows – Gréagóir Ó Dúill
Slipping Letters Beneath the Sea – Joseph Horgan
Canals of Memory – Áine Moynihan
Arthur O'Leary & Arthur Sullivan – Musical Journeys
from Kerry to the Heart of Victorian England - Bob
Fitzsimons
Crossroads – Folklore from Kerry

Real Imaginings – a Kerry anthology, edited by Tommy Frank O'Connor

Touching Stones – Liam Ryan

Where the Music Comes From – Pat Galvin

No Place Like It – Hugh O'Donnell

The Moon Canoe – Jerome Kiely

Watching Clouds – Gerry Boland

Capering Moons – Anatoly Kudryavitsky

I Shouldn't be Telling You This – Mae Leonard

Notes Towards a Love Song – Aidan Hayes

Meeting Mona Lisa – Tommy Frank O'Connor

Between the Lines – Karen O'Connor

Every DOGHOUSE book costs €12, postage free, to anywhere in the world (& other known planets). Cheques, Postal Orders (or any legal method) payable to DOGHOUSE, also PAYPAL (www.paypal.com) to doghousepaypal@eircom.net

"Buy a full set of DOGHOUSE books, in time they will be collectors' items" - Gabriel Fitzmaurice, April 12, 2005.

DOGHOUSE
P.O. Box 312
Tralee G.P.O.
Tralee
Co. Kerry
Ireland
tel + 353 6671 37547
email doghouse312@eircom.net
www.doghousebooks.ie